WOLF to WHOODLE

Liz Miles

Collins

Contents

Chapter 1 From wolves to dogs	7
Bonus: Parts of a dog	20
Chapter 2 Dogs in ancient civilisations	23
Bonus: Mythical dogs	36
Chapter 3 Medieval dogs	38
Chapter 4 Renaissance dogs	53
Bonus: Dogs in art	66
Chapter 5 Victorian dogs	69
Bonus: Dogs in books and on screen	84
Chapter 6 Dogs in the modern world	87
Bonus: Helpers around the world	102
Glossary	104
About the author	106
Book chat	108

Chapter 1
From wolves to dogs

Dogs are the most popular pet in the world. (Cats come second.) In the UK alone, there are over 12 million domesticated dogs. Domesticated means 'tamed'. Unlike wild animals, domesticated dogs can be trained so they can live with people.

Dogs have played an important part in people's lives for thousands of years, and many dog owners feel a strong connection with these loyal animals. So, what is the origin of the world's favourite pet?

Today, pet dogs come in all shapes and sizes. This a whoodle (a cross between a wheaten terrier and a poodle).

Wolf-like dogs

Scientists have worked out that dogs evolved from wolves in the distant past. The first dogs were very different from the dogs we know today. They were wolf-like and wild.

> **Fact**
>
> The scientific name for today's domestic dogs is *canis lupus familiaris*. *Canis* means dog, *lupus* means wolf and *familiaris* means domestic.

Wolf-like dogs hunted for meat. They might have looked a bit like modern-day wolves.

Prehistoric 'pets'

No one knows exactly when in prehistory wolf-like dogs became domesticated dogs. Most scientists think it happened between 35,000 and 16,000 years ago. Finding a date is complicated because domestication probably happened at different times in different places. But we do know that contact with people was the main cause.

During this period, people lived as hunters and gatherers. They hunted wild animals for food, such as deer, mammoths and antelopes. They also fished and gathered edible plants and fruits. They used simple tools, made of wood, stone and bone, and either settled or moved around in small groups.

Perhaps the wolf-like dogs were attracted to these people's left-over food. It's easy to imagine one grabbing a discarded bone. People might have encouraged the less aggressive ones to come closer by feeding them. Having wolf-like dogs nearby could keep more dangerous animals away.

Over the years, prehistoric peoples picked the wolf-like dogs that suited them best and bred them. For example, they might have chosen male and female dogs who were friendly towards people, and bred them together so that they had puppies. These puppies probably inherited their parents' friendliness. If people did this repeatedly, as time went by, each new set of puppies would have become tamer. Eventually, the puppies became completely tame. The wolf-like dogs had changed into a new type of animal: the domesticated dog.

The dogs themselves benefitted from staying with people. They were fed and protected. It was important to please people, so the dogs followed their orders. Over generations, some dogs' faces changed to look friendlier, with shorter snouts and floppy ears. Others developed **traits** that made them better helpers, such as the ability to catch prey and bring it back for their owners.

Later, when people started to settle and plant seeds to grow food, they tamed other animals as well, like sheep. Dogs developed herding skills to help keep these animals under control.

The type of wolves alive today are wild and dangerous. They can't be trained to live with people like dogs can.

Daring to domesticate

Ancient evidence shows how people found dogs very useful. Cave art from 8,000 years ago, etched into rock, shows dogs in hunting scenes. This is the oldest evidence of people putting leads on dogs.

Ancient etchings found in present-day Saudi Arabia: we know the animals are dogs and not wolves because of the standing-up ears, curly tails and short snouts.

Just like today, the leads helped these people to control and train their dogs. Their dogs probably sniffed out, looked or listened for animals for the owners to catch and eat.

The leads were tied to the hunters' waists, so their hands were free to shoot with their bows and arrows. Dogs must have been important to these people because **archaeologists** have counted around 350 dogs in their art.

Today, people use harnesses and leads to help keep dogs under control. Although many people disagree with hunting today, some still use dogs to track animals.

In the past, fox **hounds** were used to hunt for foxes in the UK. Today, fox hunting is banned.

Helping each other

Dogs definitely benefitted from their relationship with prehistoric people. Early evidence of this was found in Alaska, US. Archaeologists discovered the bone of a dog that lived 12,000 years ago. Then they found another dog's bone from over 8,000 years ago in the same area. Both bones showed a substance that's found only in salmon. This meant that the dogs had eaten a lot of salmon.

This puzzled archaeologists because at the time, wolves and dogs only hunted and ate land animals, not fish. The answer had to be that their owners had fed them! So we know these dogs were fed meals of salmon in exchange for staying with the people.

Dogs still benefit from their bonds with humans. Healthy, tasty meals are an important part of the deal!

What graves teach us

At some point in prehistory, dogs started to live with smaller family groups and form emotional bonds with their owners. The oldest evidence of people really caring for – perhaps even loving – their dogs was found in the city of Bonn, Germany.

A grave discovered in Bonn from about 14,000 years ago had the remains of a woman, a man, an older dog (which scientists think might have looked like the dog opposite – a Saluki) and a puppy. The shared grave suggests that they all lived together.

By examining the puppy's teeth, a scientist worked out that it had suffered from a deadly illness called canine distemper when it was just 19 weeks old. Yet it had lived more than seven months, which meant it must have been nursed by its owners. They probably kept it warm, cleaned up its vomit, and gave it food and water. It would have died much sooner without this care.

Luckily, today, we have vets and dog medicines.

Prehistoric dog graves are extra evidence that people cared for their dog companions.

In Spain, archaeologists found a grave-site dating back about 4,000 years, where both people and dogs were buried.

Archaeologists in Sweden found an 8,400-year-old grave of a dog in the remains of a prehistoric settlement.

The remains of the dog found in a grave in Sweden. The skeleton shows it was a bit like a big, muscular greyhound, with powerful jaws.

The fact that dogs were buried with or near prehistoric people shows how important the dogs were to them. It's likely that prehistoric people felt pain and grief when their pets died, just like many dog owners do today.

Today, lots of people bury their dogs in their gardens or in special pet cemeteries. People pay for gravestones or memorials. There are pet cemeteries in many parts of the world, such as London, England and Istanbul, Turkey.

This gravestone in Istanbul remembers a dog called Maximus Tigli.

Parts of a dog

fur for keeping warm and dry

powerful muscles

tail for communication, balance and movement

pads on paws for grip

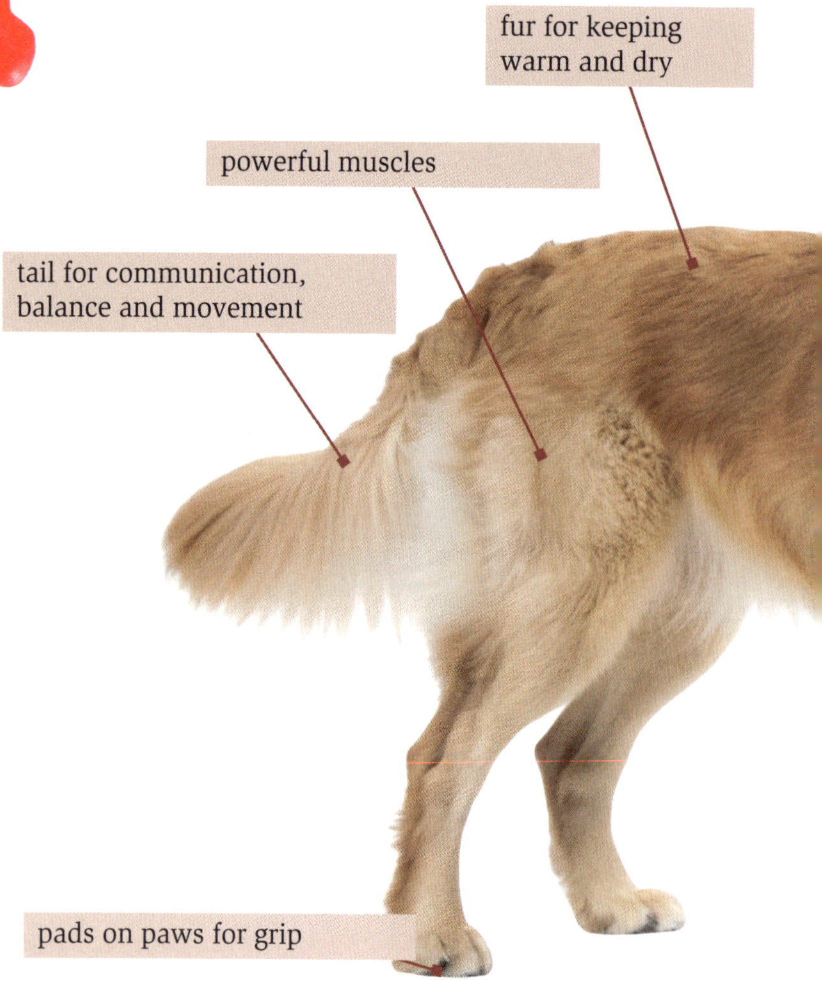

Chapter 2
Dogs in ancient civilisations

Dogs became even more important when ancient peoples started to live more complex lives and built towns and cities. Dogs often appear in the crafts, traditions, religions and beliefs of ancient **cultures**. Many ancient cultures respected dogs as companions. Some people believed that this companionship could last even after death. Some cultures worshipped dogs as gods, too.

This carving, on a tomb in ancient Egypt, is more than 2,000 years old.

This clay dog from ancient China is 2,200 years old.

Some ancient peoples began to breed dogs to do different jobs. For example, they chose male and female dogs who had longer legs, and bred them together so that they had puppies that would grow into long-legged runners. These speedy dogs helped to catch wild animals for their humans.

Ancient Egypt

Ancient Egypt is famous for its pyramids, tombs and treasures, but its many pictures and carvings of dogs are remarkable, too.

Ancient Egyptian dogs were hunters and guards, and they fought in battles. It's hard to know exactly what sort of dogs they were, but they included ancestors of today's Saluki and some greyhound breeds.

A disk from an ancient Egyptian tomb shows a fast dog chasing a gazelle. It looks like a modern-day Saluki.

It's thought that the Saluki is one of the oldest types of dog. Saluki dogs were bred in ancient Egypt for their long legs and sharp long-range sight. They were well adapted to catch speedy animals such as gazelles in the desert.

a modern-day Saluki

Afterlife

Ancient Egyptians believed that they had another life after death. They put things they might want or need in the afterlife in their tombs. Some wanted their dogs. When their dogs died, wealthy owners had their dogs' bodies **embalmed** and put in the family tomb. In this way, they hoped to meet them again in the afterlife.

an embalmed dog from an Egyptian tomb

Some families shaved off their own eyebrows as a sign of their grief at losing their pet. This showed respect and a deep bond with their dogs.

Dogs and a similar animal, the jackal, were so highly respected that they were used to represent gods. The god Anubis had a jackal's head and was believed to guide souls in the afterlife.

Anubis, from the tomb of the teenage pharaoh, Tutankhamun

Dog names

We know the names some ancient Egyptians chose for their dogs. Names appear on carvings and dog collars.

They include, translated into English: North-Wind, Brave One, and Good Herdsman. One name describes the dog's speed: 'One who is fashioned as an arrow'. Another might suggest the dog was lazy: 'Useless'.

Today, some of the most popular names for dogs in the UK and US are:

Ancient Greece

Dogs were important in ancient Greece too. They were valued in society and in families, as workers and companions. They appear on all kinds of everyday objects, such as coins and vases.

This Greek perfume container shows a woman and her dog. The bottle is at least 2,600 years old.

Some dogs in ancient Greece worked on farms. The farmers used them to protect their animals, such as sheep and goats, from wolves and other wild animals. Some farmers put a special collar on their dogs for protection. These 'wolf collars' had spikes to keep the dogs safe from a deadly bite during a wolf attack. Collars like this might have been put on dogs who were taken into battle too.

Here are some examples of spiked collars, invented by the ancient Greeks. Dangerous collars like these are not allowed to be used today.

Dogs often feature in Greek myths. Greek gods and heroes often had dogs as companions. For example, the goddess of hunting and nature, Artemis, is often shown with a hunting dog.

Ancient Greek myths include dogs that are loyal and dogs that are fearsome. The most frightening dog of all is Cerberus from the story of Heracles, an ancient Greek hero.

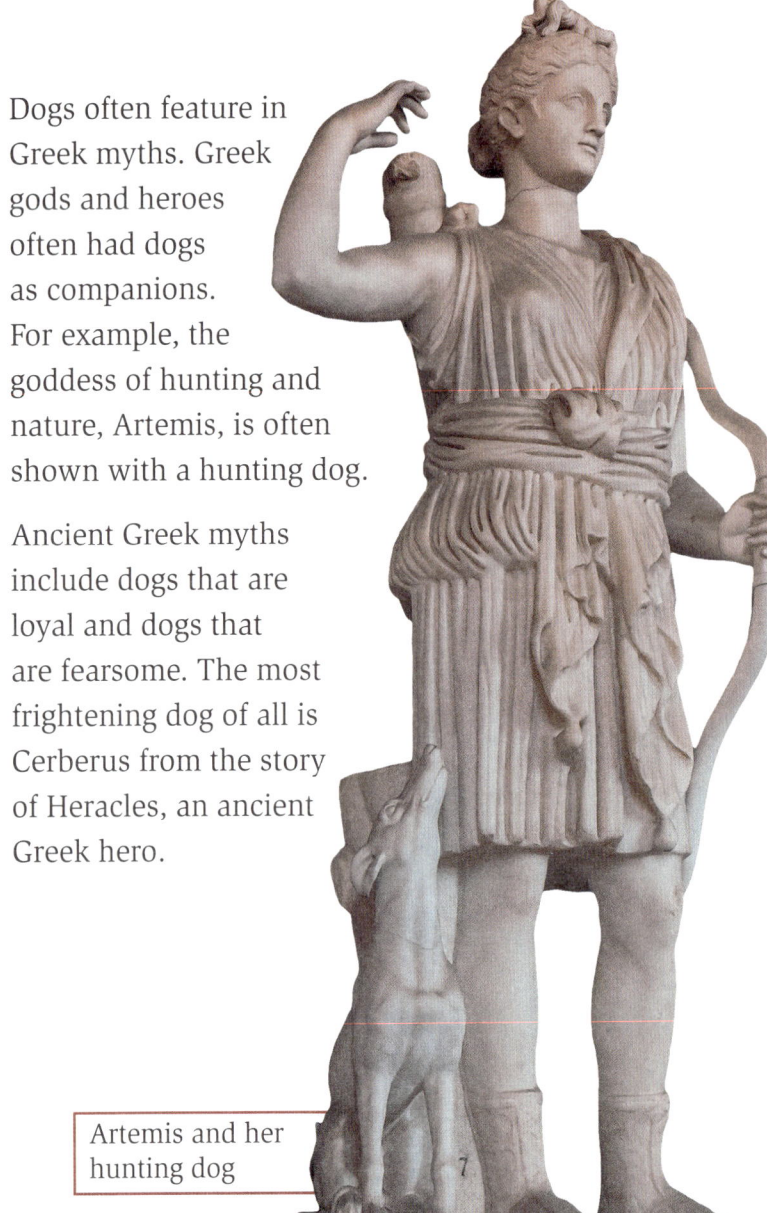

Artemis and her hunting dog

Heracles had to prove his courage by capturing Cerberus, a flesh-eating dog. It had three heads, snakes around its neck, and a tail that ended with the jaws of a dragon or serpent. It guarded the **Underworld**. After someone had died and been taken to the Underworld, Cerberus did not allow them to escape. Heracles found the dog and wrestled with it until it admitted defeat.

Heracles with Cerberus – the mythical three-headed dog

Ancient Rome

Some of the best evidence of dogs in ancient history comes from the Romans.

The town of Pompeii was buried when a volcano nearby erupted in 79 CE. Lots of details of the people's (and dogs') lives were preserved. There's evidence from artworks, too. For example, mosaics show dogs on leads, including this mosaic in a hallway.

The words in Latin (*cave canem*) mean: Beware of the dog!

We still see signs like this today!

When the Romans invaded England, they found a muscular type of dog called the Molossus, which they took back to Rome. These dogs were led into arenas such as the Colosseum. They had to fight wild animals like lions and bears, as well as gladiators.

a Molossus statue, guarding an ancient Greek tomb

Archaeologists have found skeletons of smaller dogs like the dachshund in the Colosseum. They probably entertained the crowd with tricks.

the ruins of the Colosseum where many dogs had to perform or fight

Ancient China

Domesticated dogs have been kept as companions and hunters in China for at least 24,000 years! Dogs also appear in ancient Chinese mythology. **Amulets**, showing dogs, were thought to keep their owners safe. The amulets were put in graves, too, to protect the person who had died as they passed on to an afterlife.

The Chinese calendar has a 12-year cycle. Each year is linked to an animal and its character traits. The Year of the Dog comes eleventh in the cycle. A legend explains that an emperor set a race for animals to get their place in the calendar. The dog ended up close to last because it stopped to play or bathe in a river!

The Year of the Dog

Ancient Mesoamerica (Central America)

Dogs were important to many different peoples in this area. The Aztec people believed that dogs existed before humans, so should be treated with great respect. A popular dog in Mesoamerica was hairless – a bit like today's Xolo.

an ancient clay sculpture of a Xolo dog

a modern-day Xolo dog

Aztec people also believed in a dog-headed god that guided dead souls to the Underworld. It often appeared in the form of a hairless dog.

Mythical dogs

In Greek mythology, the dog Argus became a symbol for loyalty. He waited 20 years for his master, Odysseus, to return from war.

Orion and his two hunting dogs also appear in Greek mythology. Patterns of stars in the night were named in their honour.

In Chinese mythology, the dog Tiangou is said to swallow the Moon or the Sun during eclipses.

Tales of a legendary dog called El Cadejo are told in Central America. The creature has red eyes when it attacks and blue eyes when it's resting.

Chapter 3
Medieval dogs

The medieval period in Europe lasted from the end of the Roman Empire in the 5th century to the 15th century, about 600 years ago. Written sources, art and other evidence show how some types of dog gained status and even became fashion items. Wealthy people wanted to own fashionable dogs, and often liked to show them off. However, most dog owners were poor, and most dogs lived hard lives, on farms and in towns and cities.

In this picture, a nobleman (and his dog) are presenting a book to a queen.

Castle dogs

Some dogs lived in castles and wealthy people's homes. They did all kinds of jobs. They were trained to turn wheels to draw water, and **spits** to cook meat in the kitchens.

They became messengers and guards, pets and herders. Hounds were often the most admired and valued because of their hunting skills.

Hunting hounds

In medieval England, hunting became a regular hobby for the rich and powerful. Laws set aside areas of land where only knights, nobles and the king and his friends could hunt. Having a hunting hound was a status symbol – it showed you were rich.

a medieval hunting scene, showing hounds chasing deer

Different types of dogs and hounds were bred to hunt using different methods.

Scent hounds

These were trained to quietly sniff out prey. They led their owner to animals such as deer, wild boar and rabbits. They had an exceptionally good sense of smell, like the bloodhounds we know today.

Today, bloodhounds can track a faint scent to find missing people after a disaster.

Sight and scent hounds

These chased prey in a pack, using their eyes, ears and noses. They were called greyhounds, but they varied in type and size. All had to be agile and fast runners. Similar breeds today include the small Italian greyhound and the big Irish wolfhound.

Today, people breed greyhounds for racing.

Bloodhounds came to England with invaders from Normandy, France. The Normans, led by William the Conqueror, beat the English troops in 1066. Then, William was crowned King of England. After that, bloodhounds became a fashionable status symbol.

> A famous artwork called the Bayeux Tapestry, made after the Norman invasion, includes 35 dogs! This scene shows us what a medieval hunt might have looked like.

Water dogs

Some medieval dogs were bred to **retrieve** prey. Poodles, with their thick, curly hair, were first bred in the 1300s. Hunters trained them to jump into rivers and lakes to retrieve waterfowl like ducks and geese. A special haircut helped them: short-clipped patches let their legs move easily for swimming while bulging puffs of curly hair kept them warm and afloat. Their curly hair acted like a buoyancy aid because it trapped pockets of air. The word 'poodle' derives from the German word *puddeln* which means 'to splash in water'.

Poodles' puffball haircuts today are usually for show rather than retrieving ducks!

Medieval kennels

Hunting hounds were expensive, so their owners looked after them well. Some of the first evidence of dog kennels appears in medieval records. There's written evidence that, in England, hounds were kept in kennels that were cleaned every day. The dogs were rubbed down with straw and regularly fed and watered. If hounds became ill, they had special foods such as bean broth, goat's milk and eggs.

This picture is from a medieval book on hunting, written about 600 years ago.

Fashionable dogs

It was fashionable for wealthy women to have a little dog. Paintings and sculptures show that some of their dogs were a bit like pugs.

the tomb of a lady with a small dog that might represent her favourite pet

Princes, knights and nobles had their favourite dogs, too. Their tombs often also show a dog at their feet.

Favourite hunting dogs often appear on the tombs of wealthy men.

Wealthy people's little dogs often had fancy collars with bells attached. Hunting dogs, like greyhounds, wore plainer, broader leather collars. Messenger dogs had to have a well-fitted collar to hold paper notes or letters. They often had to run through streets between home or workplaces delivering messages.

Today, little dogs are still fashionable.

Street dogs and wolves

Not all dogs were liked and many lived less happy lives on the streets of towns and cities. Most people found it hard to feed themselves, let alone a pet dog. Hungry dogs, searching for food and fighting to survive, could be aggressive. During this time, the word 'cur' was used for dangerous dogs. It comes from an older word *kurra* which means 'to growl'.

Rat-catchers' dogs

Rat catchers were employed across Europe to keep rats under control. Rats carried diseases and damaged food stores. Rat catchers trained dogs and ferrets to help catch them. Their dogs were a type of terrier.

Terriers were first bred for their instinct to sniff out animals that hid underground, like foxes and rabbits. They were small enough to dig into burrows. The name 'terrier' was first used by French owners in the Middle Ages and comes from the Latin word *terra*, meaning 'of earth'.

This painting from 1824 by Thomas Woodward is called *The Rat-Catcher and His Dogs*.

Dogs in the Plague

A **pandemic** spread across North Africa, the Middle East and Europe between 1347 and 1352. It killed millions of people.

Fleas and lice on people or fleas on rats carried the disease, but no one knew this at the time. During later outbreaks of the disease, dogs and cats were mistakenly blamed. In London, in the 'Great Plague' of 1665, people were ordered to kill dogs and cats. This meant there were fewer animals around catching and killing rats, so the numbers of rats increased.

Legendary medieval dogs

Cavall

The legendary King Arthur is said to have had a favourite loyal hound called Cavall. King Arthur and Cavall hunted a terrifying monster-like wild boar together. After their adventure, King Arthur built a pile of stones and placed a stone with Cavall's footprint on top in his honour.

Cavall might have been a Molossus, similar to a modern-day mastiff like this.

Gelert

A legend in Wales tells the story of a loyal hound, but the story doesn't end happily.

The hound, called Gelert, belonged to a prince in Wales. The prince left his faithful dog to guard over his baby. On his return, he found the baby's cot overturned. Mistakenly thinking Gelert had killed the baby, he killed his much-loved dog. He then found the baby alive and well, and a dead wolf nearby. He realised Gelert had saved the baby by killing the wolf. The prince was so upset at his mistake that he never smiled again.

a modern sculpture of Gelert

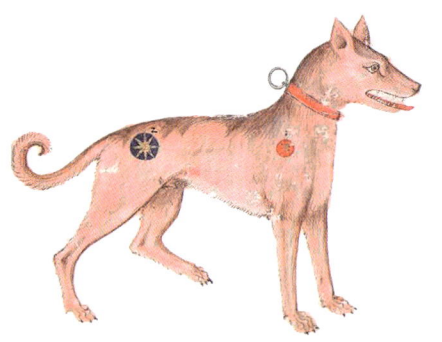

Chapter 4
Renaissance dogs

The Renaissance period came after medieval times and lasted until the end of the 1500s. We have lots of information about dogs and what people thought of them during this period. We can see dogs in paintings and read about them in plays and books.

It's clear that the luckiest dogs were usually owned by the wealthy, while most dogs still had to live on the streets. In Renaissance times, wealthy people often owned working dogs, but increasingly they also kept dogs as trustworthy companions.

Loyalty and faithfulness

Because people felt that their dogs were trustworthy, dogs became a common symbol of faithfulness and loyalty.

Important families had badges called 'coats of arms', like this one. They often included dogs as a symbol of family loyalty.

The woman in this painting is possibly writing a love letter, and the dog might symbolise her faithfulness in the love she feels. Writing love letters was common at the time.

The Letter Writer (1680) by Frans van Mieris

Special relationships

During the Renaissance, there was a 'rebirth' of ancient Roman and Greek cultures, which peaked in the 1500s. This led to a keen interest in art and realistic portrait painting. These portraits reveal a lot about the dogs owned by wealthy families, including clues about the dogs' characters, as well as their physical appearance. The portraits also tell us more about the relationships between dogs and their owners.

This portrait of a two-year-old girl from a wealthy Italian family was painted by Titian. It's from 1542 and shows Clarissa giving her pet dog a ring-shaped biscuit. She looks a bit afraid, but the caring dog seems to be trying to comfort her.

a detail from Titian's painting of Clarissa and her dog

Mary, Queen of Scots, was fond of dogs, especially spaniels and terriers. These lapdogs, like the one in the portrait below, were companions and a comfort to Mary throughout her life. While she was in prison for plotting against Elizabeth I, Queen of England, she embroidered pictures of her dogs to help pass the time and keep her spirits up. Mary was executed in 1587, and some accounts say that one of her lapdogs hid in her clothes when she went to her death.

This painting of an Italian duke by the artist Titian includes a small Maltese lapdog. In the Renaissance it was usually women, rather than men, who were painted with a lapdog. It's possible that the painting is meant to show the duke as both strong and gentle. His hand on the dog shows both the duke's authority and his gentle caring nature.

Dogs on the street

During the Renaissance, many people, rich and poor, kept powerful guard dogs outside their homes for protection against burglars and other dangers. There were no police at the time, so dogs were often the only way that people could keep themselves safe from crime. Without dog wardens or animal charities to look after strays, lots of homeless dogs ran around on the streets, semi-wild.

Guard dogs and stray dogs could be aggressive to passers-by, so dogs didn't always have the best reputation. This is reflected in how the word 'dog' is used in some Renaissance literature.

Dog words

The words 'dog' or 'cur' were often used as an insult. Shakespeare, the famous English playwright, uses the word 'dog' about 200 times in his plays. Examples of 'dog' insults in his plays are:

Dog idioms

We still use some idioms or sayings from hundreds of years ago that refer to dogs. Some show how dogs were often treated badly and left to fend for themselves. Here are some examples:

It's a dog's life.	It's a horrid life of hard work (like most dogs' lives were in the 1500s).
It's gone to the dogs.	It's become ruined/neglected.
It's a dog-eat-dog world.	People will hurt each other to succeed.

Dogs on the move

Increasing overseas travel meant that different types of dog were taken to different countries and continents.

Wealthy British people travelling abroad noticed a new breed of hound – spotted Dalmatians. They were originally hunting dogs and ran alongside their owners' horses. The English brought Dalmatians home and used them to run alongside their horse-drawn carriages instead. Travel in the 1700s was dangerous – bandits could easily stop a carriage. So the athletic Dalmatians ran alongside them, guarding the passengers and their belongings.

During the Renaissance, ships set sail from European countries to explore, and often invade, lands in America. Many European invaders stayed in order to establish **colonies**, taking land from the people who already lived there. These European explorers and settlers brought their dogs with them, for protection and hunting.

In 1620, this English man set off to North America on the *Mayflower*, with his mastiff.

Changing attitudes

In Europe, people began to challenge old ideas about dogs. The traditional view of animals was that they weren't important in themselves. They were only of value as possessions of their owners, or for the work they did. But now, people began to think that dogs and other animals were worthy of respect in their own right.

Dog portraits

In the Renaissance, dogs were usually only ever painted with people. But soon painters began to focus just on the dogs. Because dogs were now viewed as more important, more artists devoted whole paintings to them.

The lifelike portraits of dogs that began in the Renaissance continued to inspire artists to paint pictures of dogs in the years that followed.

One of the first paintings of dogs alone was by an Italian artist called Bassano. A wealthy Italian paid Bassano to paint his hunting dogs. Paying for a painting like this suggests that the man cared for and treasured his dogs. It soon became fashionable for people to pay for paintings of their much-loved pets.

Two Hunting Dogs Tied to a Tree Stump (1548–1550) is so realistic that you can sense the dogs' strength and gentleness and almost feel their soft coats and floppy ears.

We don't know who owned this little dog, but the artist was an Italian called Giovanna Garzoni, painting in the 1600s. She became well-known for painting animals and plants. The cuteness of the dog shows through, and perhaps there's humour in the nibbled pastries!

a lapdog by painter Giovanna Garzoni

The English painter George Stubbs is famous for his animal paintings in the 1700s. His first painting of a dog, *The Spanish Pointer*, shows its intelligence, liveliness and character. Above all, it inspires admiration for the dog.

The Spanish Pointer was resold in 2024 for around £2 million!

The fashion for pet portraits continues today. People can even pay to have their dogs painted or collaged in a 'Renaissance' style!

Dogs in art

Dogs appear in all kinds of art, and throughout history.

This carved hunting scene is from Mesopotamia, an ancient region in the Middle East. It is about 2,700 years old.

This statue shows a happy-looking dog. It was made in China over 2,000 years ago.

This painting is called *Paw-trait*. Dogs are often depicted as cute and funny.

An origami dog. Origami is the ancient Japanese art of paper-folding.

A colourful, modern-day statue of a dog in a park in Florida, US.

Chapter 5
Victorian dogs

In the 19th century, the **Industrial Revolution** caused a lot of changes in **Victorian** Britain. Towns and cities became overcrowded as more people moved from the countryside to work in new factories. Many working dogs had hard lives. Dogs were often mistreated, and more stray dogs lived on the streets.

There were no dog homes in early Victorian times, so stray dogs had to fend for themselves.

During this time, people started to express concern about cruelty to dogs. Queen Victoria, who reigned in the UK from 1837 to 1901, was a dog lover and became a powerful force towards improving their lives.

Queen Victoria's many pet dogs included this Pomeranian, called Turi.

Welfare worries

People started to worry about the cruel treatment of working dogs, such as the heavy loads they had to pull. During the Industrial Revolution, more food had to be taken from farms to sell in town markets. Horses were expensive, so some farmers used dogs instead of horses to pull carts.

a Victorian dog cart

The population of stray dogs continued to grow in towns. A lot of people suffered from poverty in Victorian times. They found it hard to afford to feed themselves, let alone a dog. In one year alone, over 10,000 stray dogs were found on London's streets.

This dog operated a contraption that worked a sewing machine!

The increasing concern for the welfare of dogs in Victorian times led to new charities and laws.

In 1824, a group of people concerned about animal welfare met in London, and their discussions led to the founding of the RSPCA (Royal Society for the Prevention of Cruelty to Animals).

The RSPCA and Princess Victoria pushed for laws that banned cruelty towards dogs at work and in homes.

At last, the government did pass laws in 1835. They banned cruelty to dogs and other domestic animals in the UK.

The charity gained the word 'Royal' when Queen Victoria, aged 21 years old, became its patron in 1840.

In 1839, there was a specific ban on the use of dogs to pull heavy loads in London. Later, in 1845, the ban was extended nationwide. Queen Victoria helped push a law through that banned **muzzles** (except on savage dogs) and worked to stop the clipping of dogs' tails or ears, which was common at the time.

Charles Dickens, the Victorian novelist, was another passionate dog lover and supported the RSPCA.

Dog homes

People who cared about dogs urgently wanted to help stray dogs – as well as lost dogs who had become separated from their owners.

In 1860, the world's first dog home was founded, called The Temporary Home for Lost and Starving Dogs. It later became today's Battersea Dogs Home in London. Stray dogs were taken there and rehomed. Sometimes, lost dogs were reunited with their owners.

an RSPCA poster from the 1930s

Battersea Dogs Home in London in 1886

This postcard celebrates the reunion of an owner and their lost dog.

Never forgotten

Dogs as pets became increasingly popular during Victorian times and the bonds between owners and their dogs strengthened. After a dog's death, some owners wanted to bury their dogs in a special place. As a result, the first modern pet cemeteries appeared, where dogs were buried and gravestones were placed in their honour.

One of the first Victorian pet graveyards appeared in Hyde Park in London. A man asked the park-keeper whether his pet dog, Cherry, could be buried there because she had loved her walks in the park. After the keeper agreed to the burial, the news spread, and more people asked to bury their dogs there too.

In the 1800s, dog memorials and statues became increasingly popular. In 1872, a statue of a Skye terrier called Bobby was placed in front of Greyfriars cemetery in Edinburgh, Scotland, a year after the dog died.

He was known as Greyfriars Bobby because for 14 years he sat every day in Greyfriars churchyard, beside his master's grave.

Bobby

Standard breeds

The Victorians' admiration for dogs led to an interest in different breeds of dog. Until the 1800s, it was hard to clearly name or define types of dogs because no rules or descriptions had been agreed. For example, dogs described as greyhounds could look very different. In Victorian times, dog breeders used strict selective breeding to create and define standard breeds of dog.

The Victorians defined and registered many breeds for the first time, such as the Irish Wolfhound in 1886.

What is 'selective breeding'?

Selective breeding means choosing certain dogs to breed so that puppies with specific traits are born. This is how it's done:

- First, the breeder decides on certain dog traits (like a short tail, curly hair and gentle temperament).

- Next, they choose parent dogs with the best of those traits and put them together to breed. The offspring (puppies) with the best of those traits are again chosen as parent dogs to breed.

- Generation after generation of dogs are selected in this way, until at last all the puppies from a pair have the required traits.

Dog shows

People became very proud of their carefully bred dogs, and dog shows became popular. The first national dog show was held in Victorian England in 1870. Then, in 1873, the world's first Kennel Club was formed to provide a set of rules for these competitions. The rules encouraged people to look after the health of their dogs, and vets checked the dogs at shows.

winners at the 1892 dog show at Crystal Palace, London

Crufts

In 1891, Charles Cruft, who worked for Spratt's pet food company, organised the first Crufts dog show. Spratt's made the first ever dog food. The Crufts dog show is now an international dog show, run by the Kennel Club in the UK.

Charles Cruft

Dogs in literature

Throughout the Victorian times, writers wrote proudly about their dogs and often described them as friends.

English poet Elizabeth Barrett Browning wrote a poem called *To Flush, My Dog* in 1844. In the poem, she praises her cocker spaniel's patience and affection, and describes it as a 'Loving friend' with 'tasselled ears' and a 'friendly voice'.

We can see from Victorian stories how dogs became members of the family, and were seen as brave, clever and loyal. More people had better jobs after the Industrial Revolution, and so more families could afford to keep pet dogs.

In *Alice in Wonderland* (1865) Alice plays with a puppy when she shrinks to a tiny size.

Just three years after the death of Queen Victoria, J.M. Barry's story of Peter Pan came out. The dog called Nana acts as a member of the family, and looks after the children, a bit like a nanny.

Bonus

Dogs in books and on screen

Dogs appear in lots of well-known children's stories.

Toto is Dorothy's pet dog in *The Wonderful Wizard of Oz* by L. Frank Baum (1900) and the film version (1939).

The One Hundred and One Dalmatians novel by Dodie Smith (1956) was made into lots of successful film versions. The author owned nine Dalmatians as pets.

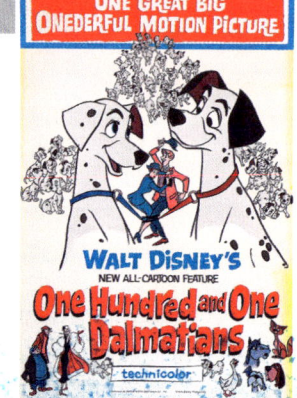

The Incredible Journey (1961) by Sheila Burnford tells the story of a 480-kilometre journey by two dogs and a cat, back to their master.

Hairy Maclary from Donaldson's Dairy (1983) by Lynley Dodd is a classic rhyming book for children. As well as Hairy Maclary, it features dogs called Bottomley Potts and Schnitzel von Krumm.

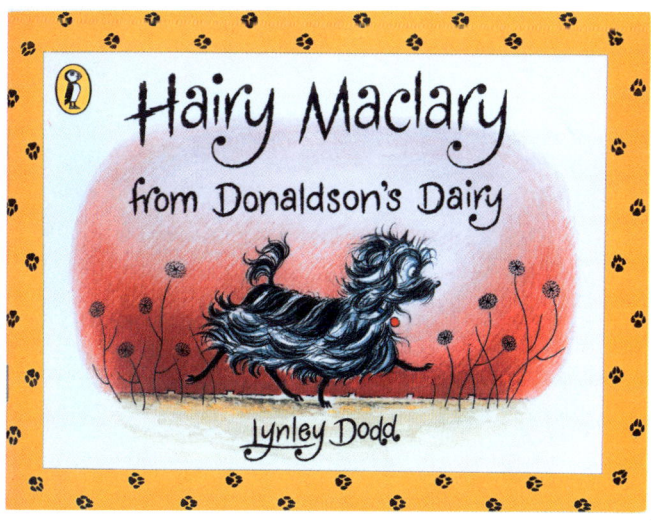

Chapter 6
Dogs in the modern world

In recent times, dogs have learnt how to help human beings in new ways. The bond between human and dog has deepened.

This dog has been trained to comfort people.

Wartime helpers

In the 20th century, two world wars affected the lives of dogs as well as their owners. Dogs did lots of jobs during the wars.

First World War dogs

In the First World War, thousands of dogs were trained by armies. There were no modern communications, like mobile phones, so trained dogs carried messages across battlefields. Ambulance dogs found wounded soldiers and took them to safety.

Ambulance dogs carried first-aid kits.

A wartime star

At the end of the First World War, an American soldier rescued some puppies in Germany. One puppy, Rin Tin Tin, became a movie star after the soldier took him back to the US. Rin Tin Tin appeared in nearly 30 movies. He visited hospitals and schools, signing his photo with a paw print.

Second World War dogs

In the Second World War, most countries' armies used dogs as messengers and to listen out for the approaching enemy. The dogs were trained to silently point with their noses if they picked up a scent. Dogs searched for signs of life in bombed buildings.

a dog helps rescuers in London

Judy

Some dogs, like Judy, received medals for bravery. During the Second World War, Judy saved many people's lives, survived being onboard sinking ships and spent years as a prisoner of war.

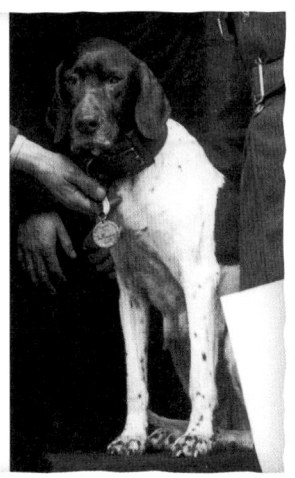

Always learning

Dogs often seem to enjoy learning new skills and tricks, and training a dog deepens the bond between dog and owner.

Over the last 50 years, people learnt a lot about how to train dogs. Dog trainers showed how the best method was to give dogs rewards for good behaviour. Consistency, compassion and patience were vital too.

Television programmes over the last few decades about badly behaved dogs show how the owners are sometimes at fault. Once they use the right training method, 'bad dogs' soon become good.

Competitions

Agility competitions test dogs' accuracy and speed as they race around a course of obstacles and jumps. They test not just the dogs but the owners too, who guide their dogs around the course.

The first agility competition was held at the Crufts dog show in 1978. In 1980, the Kennel Club made rules for the sport. It still offers advice on how to train dogs for agility safely.

Dogs must speed around up to 20 obstacles in less than a minute!

International sheepdog trials have shown how clever dogs are, too. Sheepdog trial competitions involve dogs herding sheep into a specific place as quickly as possible. The competitions began in New Zealand in the 1860s, but are now held all around the world.

The sheepdogs, such as border collies, are specially bred to be herders. They control the sheep by running around the flock. They also control the herd by lying down and staring. This intimidates the sheep.

Assistance dogs

Dogs help people in lots of ways. In recent years, they have been trained to be assistance dogs and to work with professional teams, such as emergency rescuers, doctors and the police.

Assistance dogs go to live with people who have, for example, disabilities and medical conditions. They are trained to help with their specific needs.

Guide dogs help people who have a visual impairment, such as blindness. They help their owners move around safely, for example, helping them to avoid obstacles and safely cross roads.

Guide dogs are a type of assistance dog.

The first guide dog school opened in 1916, during the First World War. Hundreds of soldiers were returning home with sight injuries, and a German doctor noticed how a dog was trying to look after one of his blind patients in the hospital grounds. This inspired the doctor to work out how to train guide dogs and open the school.

Hearing dogs help people with hearing loss. They are trained to alert their owner to important sounds, such as the ring of a doorbell or telephone.

Golden retrievers are often assistance dogs because they have a calm and friendly nature.

Other assistance dogs include dogs that help people with stress or anxiety. Some dogs help children to feel more confident. Today, dogs often help out in libraries and schools.

Dogs are good listeners.

When assistance dogs aren't working, they live with their owner like any other family pet. In the UK alone, it's thought that there are well over 7,000 assistance dogs.

Emergency dogs

Dogs around the world are now trained to help in all sorts of emergencies. Using their excellent sense of smell and sharp hearing, they can find and rescue people after storms, avalanches and earthquakes.

For hundreds of years, St Bernard dogs were known for finding and rescuing people in snowy mountains.

a St Bernard dog at work

Today, more agile dogs are members of mountain rescue teams.

Dogs have such a good sense of smell, they can pick up the scent of people buried deep in the snow.

Medical alarms

Some dogs are specially trained to assist people with certain medical conditions. They can detect whether their owner might need a medicine or emergency help. Then they help or sound an alarm.

Recent research suggests that dogs can pick up tiny scents from diseases in people's bodies. If dogs can be trained to detect early stages of a disease, doctors will be able to save more lives. This is perhaps one of the best ways in which dogs can help us!

Crimebusters

Long ago, policemen took their own pet dogs to work to help keep themselves safe. The first professional police dogs started work over 100 years ago. Since then, police dogs have become highly trained and help to solve crimes and track down criminals. Sniffer dogs are trained to pick up specific scents. They can find lots of different things, from hidden mobile phones to stolen cash.

Award winners

A pet charity called the PDSA gives medals to animals for their outstanding roles in society. A dog called Buster won a medal for his life-saving sniffer skills in the British army. A dog called Hurricane received a medal for grabbing an intruder who was trying to sneak into the US president's home.

Buster

Hurricane

Crimebusters

Long ago, policemen took their own pet dogs to work to help keep themselves safe. The first professional police dogs started work over 100 years ago. Since then, police dogs have become highly trained and help to solve crimes and track down criminals. Sniffer dogs are trained to pick up specific scents. They can find lots of different things, from hidden mobile phones to stolen cash.

Award winners

A pet charity called the PDSA gives medals to animals for their outstanding roles in society. A dog called Buster won a medal for his life-saving sniffer skills in the British army. A dog called Hurricane received a medal for grabbing an intruder who was trying to sneak into the US president's home.

Buster

Hurricane

Molly, a cocker spaniel dog, also won a medal from the PDSA. Her owner, Lucy, had a medical condition that limited what she could do. Molly assisted with everyday tasks, from helping with the washing to untying Lucy's shoelaces.

Given the work and help dogs now provide us, it's no wonder that dogs are greatly admired today.

Helpers around the world

Italy: a dog training to be a lifeguard

Malawi: dogs searching for survivors after a flood

Greenland: husky dogs helping to pull a sled across the ice

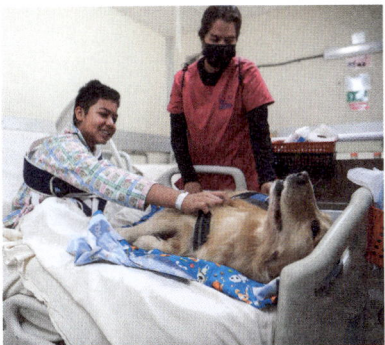
Mexico: an assistance dog comforting a hospital patient

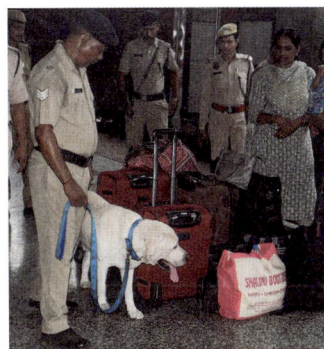
India: a security dog checking baggage

Chile: dogs herding sheep

Glossary

amulets small objects that people carry or wear to protect them from bad luck

archaeologists people who study history and prehistory by looking at objects that have been left behind

colonies areas of land taken over by another country

cultures the arts, ideas, traditions and beliefs of a group of people

embalmed preserved

hounds dogs bred to hunt

Industrial Revolution a time of great change that began over 200 years ago, when many people moved from the country to towns to work in big factories

muzzles little cages that are placed over dogs' noses and mouths to prevent them biting people or other animals

pandemic a disease that affects many people over a wide area

retrieve collect and bring back

spits rods that turn meat so it cooks evenly

traits characteristics or tendencies

Underworld a place in ancient myths where the dead go

Victorian belonging to the period of Queen Victoria's reign (1837–1901)

About the author

Did you always want to be an author?

At first, I wanted to be a teacher or an artist. Then, a very inspiring teacher at school helped me realise how exciting writing can be. She showed me how, by just starting to write, words can become sentences, and sentences can become new thoughts, new ideas and even new worlds.

Liz Miles

What was the best, and most challenging, thing about writing this book?

The best thing was being able to spend weeks reading and thinking about one of my favourite subjects – dogs! I loved finding about their history, and how they became domesticated. The most challenging thing about writing the book was deciding what I could fit into the pages, and what I had to leave out. I'm sure readers will know lots of dog stories or information that I haven't been able to squeeze in!

What type of books are your favourite to write?

All types of books are my favourites! I love writing non-fiction books because I want to share the amazing things that I've discovered through research. I also love writing stories because they can sweep us away into the lives of other characters and worlds. The facts I discover while writing non-fiction often inspire the stories I write, too.

Why did you want to write this book?
While writing history books, I noticed how dogs pop up across all centuries and places around the world. I wanted to find out more and share how important dogs have been to people for thousands and thousands of years.

Do you have a dog?
Sadly, my Tibetan terrier died but I have lots of very happy memories of him. He loved running beside rivers and the sea. Now, I help look after family and friends' dogs, including a lively Labradoodle called Ziggy and cuddly Pomeranian called Fox.

Do you have a favourite breed of dog?
I like all breeds of dog, as well as dogs that aren't any special breed at all! For me, the temperament of a dog is the most important thing, and whether they need special care. Some of the best dogs I've met are rehomed, mixed-breed dogs.

What's the best thing you learnt while writing this book?
Perhaps the best or funniest thing I learnt is that an ancient Egyptian called their dog 'Useless'. I wonder what Useless thought of their owner. It has given me an idea for a very funny story!

What do you hope readers will get from this book?
I hope readers finish the book feeling that dogs are very special. After finding out how dogs have been helping people for thousands of years, I ended up loving and respecting them more than ever. Dogs have put up with a lot, and still do, but they continue to be our helpers and loving companions when we are kind to them.

Book chat

What do you think of the book's title?

Do you have a favourite dog from the book?

What did you already know about dogs?

Have you ever seen a working dog?

What did you learn while reading this book?

> Have you ever seen a dog agility show?

> Have you ever seen dogs in art, on a screen or in a book?

> If you could see any dog from this book, which one would you choose?

> Who would you recommend this book to and why?

Was there anything in this book that really surprised you?

Would you want to have a dog as a pet? If so, which one? And if not, why not?

If you could ask the author anything, what would you ask?

Do you have or know anyone with a dog?

What's your favourite picture in the book and why do you like it?

How would you summarise this book in one sentence?

If you had to think of an alternative title for this book, what would you choose?

Book challenge:

Draw any animal of your choice in 'Renaissance' style.

Published by Collins
An imprint of HarperCollins*Publishers*

The News Building
1 London Bridge Street
London
SE1 9GF
UK

Macken House
39/40 Mayor Street Upper
Dublin 1
D01 C9W8
Ireland

© HarperCollins*Publishers* Limited 2025

10 9 8 7 6 5 4 3 2 1

ISBN 978-0-00-879619-8

All rights reserved. No part of this publication may be reproduced, stored in a retrieval system, or transmitted in any form by any means, electronic, mechanical, photocopying, recording or otherwise, without the prior written permission of the Publisher or a licence permitting restricted copying in the United Kingdom issued by the Copyright Licensing Agency Ltd, 5th Floor, Shackleton House, 4 Battle Bridge Lane, London SE1 2HX.

Without limiting the exclusive rights of any author, contributor or the publisher of this publication, any unauthorised use of this publication to train generative artificial intelligence (AI) technologies is expressly prohibited. HarperCollins also exercise their rights under Article 4(3) of the Digital Single Market Directive 2019/790 and expressly reserve this publication from the text and data mining exception.

British Library Cataloguing-in-Publication Data
A catalogue record for this publication is available from the British Library.

Download the teaching notes and word cards to accompany this book at:
http://littlewandle.org.uk/signupfluency/

Get the latest Collins Big Cat news at
collins.co.uk/collinsbigcat

Author: Liz Miles
Publisher: Laura White
Product managers: Caroline Green and Holly Woolnough
Series editor: Charlotte Raby
Development editor: Catherine Baker
Commissioning editor: Suzannah Ditchburn
Project manager: Emily Hooton
Copyeditor: Sally Byford
Proofreader: Catherine Dakin
Cover designer: Sarah Finan
Typesetter: 2Hoots Publishing Services Ltd
Production controller: Sophie Waeland

Printed in the UK.

MIX
Paper | Supporting responsible forestry
FSC™ C007454

This book contains FSC™ certified paper and other controlled sources to ensure responsible forest management.

For more information visit: www.harpercollins.co.uk/green

Made with responsibly sourced paper and vegetable ink

Scan to see how we are reducing our environmental impact.

Acknowledgements
The publishers gratefully acknowledge the permission granted to reproduce the copyright material in this book. Every effort has been made to trace copyright holders and to obtain their permission for the use of copyright material. The publishers will gladly receive any information enabling them to rectify any error or omission at the first opportunity.

Front cover Volodymyr Burdiak/Shutterstock, p7 Marie Vanderweide-Murray/Getty Images, p12 Richard Mortel/Creative Commons 2.0, p14 Pictures Now/Alamy, p19 Anadolu/Getty Images, p23l rhkamen/Getty Images, p23r Chu Yong/Getty Images, p24 Alain Guilleux/Alamy, p25 Jackie Bale/Getty Images, p26t Photo12/Getty Images, p26b Smith Archive/Alamy, p28 PHAS/Getty Images, p29 Maurice Crooks/Alamy, p32t Universal History Archive/Getty Images, p33t DEA/G. DAGLI ORTI/Getty Images, p35tr Alexey Kuznetsov/Alamy, p37t The History Collection/Alamy, p39 steeve-x-art/Alamy, p41 Pictures Now/Alamy, p45 Heritage Images/Getty Images, p46t Peter Horree/Alamy, p46b Alex Ramsay/Alamy, p49 Artefact/Alamy, p51 Nathaniel Noir/Alamy, p54t Jansos/Alamy, p54b Peter van Evert/Alamy, p55 Pictorial Press Ltd/Alamy, p56 Chronicle/Alamy, p57 ART Collection/Alamy, p60 Chronicle/Alamy, p61 Bettmann/Getty Images, p63 Carlo Bollo/Alamy, p64 VTR/Alamy, p65t Artefact/Alamy, p66t DEA/G. DAGLI ORTI/Getty Images, p67t Historical Picture Archive/Getty Images, p69 Historical Images Archive/Alamy, p70 Smith Archive/Alamy, p71 Pump Park Vintage Photography/Alamy, p72 Chronicle/Alamy, p73 UniversalImagesGroup/Getty Images, p75t Chronicle/Alamy, p75 Paul Keevil/Mary Evans Picture Library, p81b Chronicle/Alamy, p83t Buyenlarge/Getty Images, p83b Lebrecht Music & Arts/Alamy, p84t MGM Studios/Getty Images, p84b LMPC/Getty Images, p85b Kay Roxby/Alamy, p89t Pictorial Press Ltd/Alamy, p94 Brian Mitchell/Getty Images, p96 kali9/Getty Images, p97t Chronicle/Alamy, p98 ZUMA Press, Inc./Alamy, p100l PA Images/Alamy, p100r Daniel Leal/Getty Images, p102b Amos Gumlira/Getty Images, p103t Joana Kruse/Alamy. All other photos – Shutterstock